BARYONYX

A Buddy Book
by
Michael P. Goecke

ABDO
Publishing Company

VISIT US AT
www.abdopublishing.com

Published by ABDO Publishing Company, 4940 Viking Drive, Edina, Minnesota 55435.

Copyright © 2007 by Abdo Consulting Group, Inc. International copyrights reserved in all countries. No part of this book may be reproduced in any form without written permission from the publisher. Buddy Books™ is a trademark and logo of ABDO Publishing Company.

Printed in the United States.

Edited by: Sarah Tieck
Graphic Design: Denise Esner
Cover Art: Luis Rey, title page
Interior Photos/Illustrations: Pages 5 & 19: John Sibbick; pages 6, 7, 11 & 17: Natural History Museum; pages 9, 10, 13 & 20: Photos.com; page 15: Luis Rey; page 22: ©Julius T. Csotonyi; page 25: AFP/Getty Images.

Library of Congress Cataloging-in-Publication Data

Goecke, Michael P., 1968-
    Baryonyx / Michael P. Goecke.
        p. cm. — (Dinosaurs)
    Includes index.
    ISBN-13: 978-1-59928-694-5
    ISBN-10: 1-59928-694-7
    1. Baryonyx—Juvenile literature. I. Title.

QE862.S3G598 2007
567.912—dc22

                                                      2006032067

TABLE OF CONTENTS

What Was It? 4

How Did It Move? 6

Why Was It Special? 8

Land Of The Baryonyx 12

What Did It Eat? 14

What Else Lived There? 18

The Baryonyx Family 22

Discovery 24

Where Are They Today? 28

Baryonyx 29

Web Sites 30

Important Words 31

Index 32

WHAT WAS IT?

The world was a very different place 125 million years ago. Back then, dinosaurs walked the earth. One type of dinosaur was called Baryonyx.

The Baryonyx was a theropod dinosaur. This means that it walked on two legs and ate meat. It had a long, straight neck and a long tail.

The Baryonyx lived in what is now England. It was about 32 feet (10 m) long and weighed about 4,000 pounds (1,800 kg). It was known for its claws and sharp teeth. Some scientists say the Baryonyx looked like a crocodile.

Baryonyx
bar-ree-ON-ihks

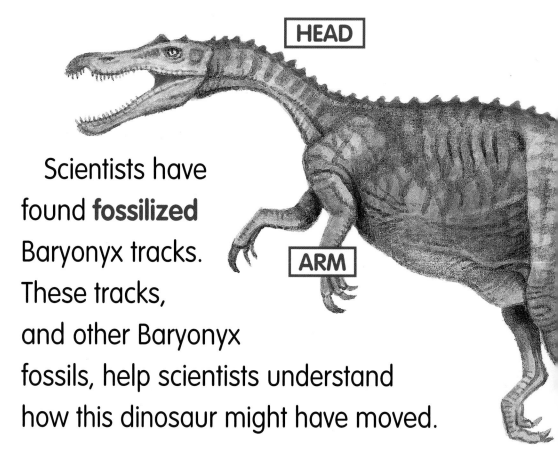

HEAD

ARM

FOOT

Scientists have found **fossilized** Baryonyx tracks. These tracks, and other Baryonyx fossils, help scientists understand how this dinosaur might have moved.

6

Scientists say the Baryonyx probably walked on its legs most of the time. It spent much of its life around water, looking for fish to eat.

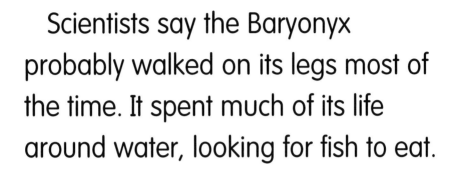

TAIL

LEG

Sometimes the Baryonyx moved around on both its arms and legs. But, when it needed to move faster, it ran on its legs.

HY WAS IT SPECIAL?

The Baryonyx was a **dangerous predator**. Its name means "heavy claw." This refers to the 12-inch (31-cm) long sharp claws it has on each hand.

Scientists compare these claws to bear claws. Bears use their claws to catch salmon.

Like grizzly bears today, the Baryonyx used its claws to catch fish.

9

The Baryonyx was a **carnivore**. It had more teeth than most other carnivorous dinosaurs. It had 64 teeth on its lower jaw and 32 on top!

Some scientists say the Baryonyx's mouth and head were much like a crocodile's.

The Baryonyx used its claws and teeth as powerful weapons.

With bearlike claws and a crocodile-like mouth, the Baryonyx was a skilled hunter.

LAND OF THE BARYONYX

The Baryonyx lived in what is now known as Europe. It roamed the land during the Early **Cretaceous period**. This was about 125 million years ago.

The earth was undergoing many changes during this time. Scientists believe the **continents** were closer together than they are today.

But when the Baryonyx lived, the continents were slowly moving apart. Scientists think this caused many volcano eruptions and **earthquakes**.

During the Early **Cretaceous period**, the earth was warm and wet. There were many lakes, rivers, and oceans. This was good for the Baryonyx because it hunted fish.

Throughout the years, volcanoes have helped shape and form the earth.

WHAT DID IT EAT?

Scientists are almost certain that the Baryonyx ate fish. It most likely ate other things, too. But, its special teeth and claws tell us that its main diet was fish. The Baryonyx probably spent its time hunting fish in lakes and streams.

The Baryonyx hunted fish in shallow water.

Scientists think the Baryonyx may have also eaten smaller dinosaurs. One **fossil** find proved this.

Scientists discovered fossilized remains of a young Iguanodon in a Baryonyx's stomach. An Iguanodon is another dinosaur that lived during the same time as the Baryonyx.

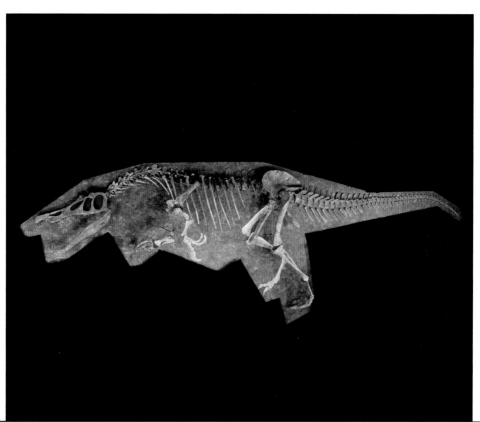

Scientists learn important information from fossil discoveries. That is how we know the eating habits of the Baryonyx.

The Iguanodon was one of the Baryonyx's prey. Its **fossils** were among the first ever discovered. Iguanodon means "iguana tooth."

The Iguanodon had a spikelike claw on each of its hands. Scientists say this dinosaur used these claws to gather food and defend itself.

An Iguanodon with its young.

The Iguanodon was about 30 feet (nine m) long. And, it weighed about as much as two hippopotamuses. That is about 10,000 pounds (4,500 kg)!

Iguanodons had teeth similar to those of today's iguanas.

THE BARYONYX FAMILY

Scientists claim that the Baryonyx was an ancestor of the Spinosaurus. This means the Baryonyx existed at an earlier time.

Scientists believe some of the bones on the Spinosaurus's back stuck up like a sail.

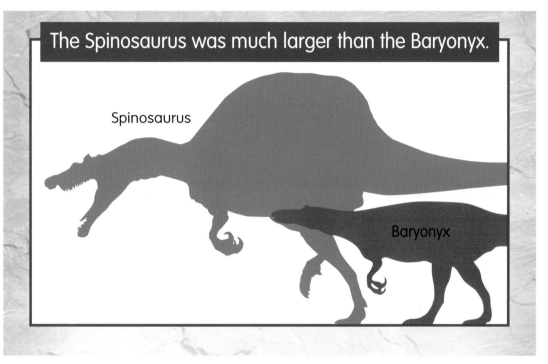

The Spinosaurus was much larger than the Baryonyx.

Spinosaurus

Baryonyx

Spinosaurus was possibly the largest **predator** ever. It was 60 feet (18 m) long and stood 20 feet (six m) high. The Spinosaurus may have weighed as much as 18,000 pounds (8,165 kg)!

DISCOVERY

In 1983, **fossil** hunter William Walker discovered the first Baryonyx fossils. He found them in a clay pit in Surrey, England. In 1986, scientists Angela C. Milner and Alan J. Charig studied these fossils and named the Baryonyx dinosaur.

Scientists must carefully remove fossils from the earth to keep them from breaking.

Other Baryonyx **fossils** have been discovered in Spain. Today, these fossils are located thousands of miles apart. But, scientists say long ago these dinosaurs all lived around the same area.

The earth's **continents** have moved since the Early **Cretaceous period**. These fossil finds have helped scientists better understand how the earth has changed since the Baryonyx lived.

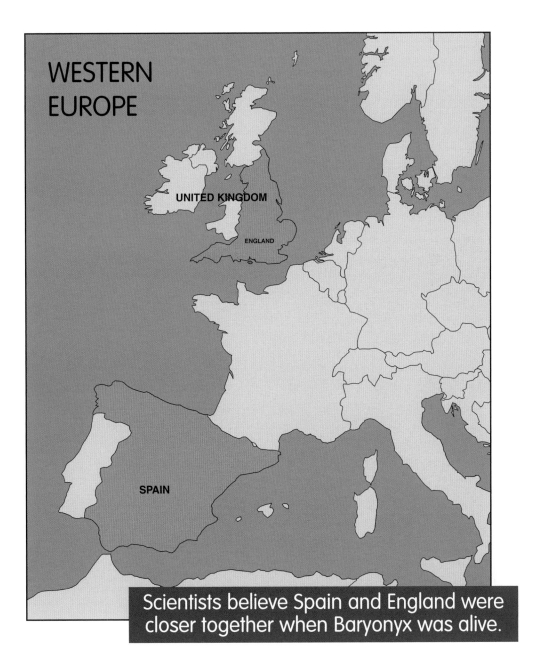

WESTERN
EUROPE

UNITED KINGDOM

ENGLAND

SPAIN

Scientists believe Spain and England were closer together when Baryonyx was alive.

27

Natural History Museum, London
Cromwell Road
London, United Kingdom SW7 5BD
http://www.nhm.ac.uk

BARYONYX

NAME MEANS	Heavy claw
DIET	Meat, fish
WEIGHT	4,000 pounds (1,800 kg)
LENGTH	32 feet (10 m)
TIME	Early Cretaceous period
SPECIAL FEATURE	Huge fishing claws
FOSSILS FOUND	Western Europe

The Baryonyx lived 125 million years ago.

The first humans appeared 1.6 million years ago.

Triassic Period	Jurassic Period	Cretaceous Period	Tertiary Period
245 Million years ago	208 Million years ago	144 Million years ago	65 Million years ago
Mesozoic Era			Cenozoic Era

WEB SITES

To learn more about the Baryonyx, visit ABDO Publishing Company on the World Wide Web. Web sites about the Baryonyx are featured on our "Book Links" page. These links are routinely monitored and updated to provide the most current information available.

www.abdopublishing.com

carnivore a meat-eater.

continent one of the earth's seven main land areas.

Cretaceous period a period of time that happened 144–65 million years ago.

dangerous something that could hurt or harm.

fossil remains of very old animals and plants commonly found in the ground. A fossil can be a bone, a footprint, or any trace of life.

predator an animal that hunts and eats other animals.

arms **6, 7**

bear **8, 9, 10**

carnivore **10**

Charig, Alan J. **24**

claws **5, 8, 9, 11, 14, 18**

Cretaceous period **12, 13, 26**

crocodile **5, 10, 11**

England **5, 24, 27**

feet **6**

fossil **6, 16, 17, 24, 25, 26**

head **6, 10**

hippopotamus **20**

iguana **20**

Iguanodon **16, 18, 19, 20**

legs **4, 7**

Milner, Angela C. **24**

neck **4**

scientists **5, 6, 7, 8, 10, 12, 14, 16, 17, 18, 22, 24, 25 26, 27**

Spain **26, 27**

Spinosaurus **22, 23**

tail **4, 7**

teeth **5, 10, 11, 14, 20**

theropod **4**

Walker, William **24**